SPOTLIGHT ON SOCIAL AND EMOTIONAL LEARNING

UNDERSTANDING POINTS OF VIEW

PERSPECTIVE-TAKING

CHRISTINE HONDERS

PowerKiDS press™

NEW YORK

Published in 2020 by The Rosen Publishing Group, Inc.
29 East 21st Street, New York, NY 10010

Editor: Rachel Gintner
Designer: Michael Flynn

Photo Credits: Cover asiseeit/E+/Getty Images; cover, pp. 1, 3–4, 6, 8–10, 12, 14–16, 18, 20–24 (background) TairA/Shutterstock.com; p. 5 Syda Productions/Shutterstock.com; p. 7 momentimages/Getty Images; p. 8 Kotin/Shutterstock.com; p. 9 AFP/Getty Images; p. 11 New Africa/Shutterstock.com; p. 12 Alias Ching/Shutterstock.com; p. 13 LWA/The Image Bank/Getty Images; p. 14 Roman Bodnarchuk/Shutterstock.com; p. 15 Veja/Shutterstock.com; p. 17 SolStock/E+/Getty Images; pp. 19, 20 Monkey Business Images/Shutterstock.com; p. 21 Visoot Uthairam/Moment/Getty Images; p. 22 https://commons.wikimedia.org/wiki/File:2018_March_For_Our_Lives_30.jpg.

Library of Congress Cataloging-in-Publication Data

Names: Honders, Christine, author.
Title: Understanding points of view : perspective-taking / Christine Honders.
Description: New York : PowerKids Press, [2020] | Series: Spotlight on social and emotional learning | Includes index.
Identifiers: LCCN 2018059216| ISBN 9781725306998 (pbk.) | ISBN 9781725307025 (library bound) | ISBN 9781725307001 (6 pack)
Subjects: LCSH: Social perception--Juvenile literature. | Perspective (Philosophy)--Juvenile literature.
Classification: LCC HM1041 .H66 2020 | DDC 302/.12--dc23
LC record available at https://lccn.loc.gov/2018059216

Manufactured in the United States of America

CPSIA Compliance Information: Batch #CW20PK. For further information contact Rosen Publishing, New York, New York at 1-800-237-9932.

CONTENTS

CHAPTER ONE

EVERYONE IS DIFFERENT

Everyone is different. Some people have brown hair. Some have yellow hair. Some have dark skin, and others have light skin. We're aware of these differences because we can see them. But what about the differences we can't see?

We can't read minds, so it's impossible to know exactly what other people are thinking. Just because someone looks like you doesn't mean they think like you. Have you ever told a joke that you thought was funny, but your friend didn't laugh? You might have thought they'd think it was funny, too. But maybe something in that joke made your friend upset or angry. No matter how alike you are, your friend's personal experiences may mean they see things differently. Being able to understand that people think and act differently even when they're in similar situations is called having **perspective**.

Having perspective is very important when you're talking with friends. It helps you understand that even though you like each other, you may not agree on everything.

CHAPTER TWO

WHAT'S PERSPECTIVE-TAKING?

Perspective-taking is a person's ability to see things through another person's point of view. That means putting yourself in someone else's shoes and understanding how they feel and why. You might think about how you'd act in a situation and why it's different from how they're acting.

When you understand other people's perspectives, you begin to understand why other people do what they do. You see that it's important to consider other people's feelings. You might change your behavior so you don't hurt others. You think very carefully about how you say something before saying it.

Kids who have trouble understanding others' perspectives may seem selfish, which means they seem to think only about themselves. They don't worry about hurting other people's feelings. It can be hard to be friends with someone like that. People like this may have trouble making and keeping friends.

If it's your birthday and your family throws you a surprise party, you're going to act in a different way from the other party guests. You'll be surprised, but the other guests won't be because they knew about the party.

CHAPTER THREE

ME FIRST!

Psychologist Jean Piaget was famous for studying **cognitive** growth in children. He said babies have only one perspective: their own. They believe the whole world centers on them. They think that other people exist just to take care of them.

Very small children see the world through their eyes alone. Everything is "me first" because they don't understand that other kids might want to be first, too. Every toy is theirs because they're the only person in the world who matters.

Jean Piaget, a Swiss psychologist, studied how children learn. He explained children's habits. His work changed the way kids are taught in school today.

When they're two or three years old, children begin to realize that other people have different **emotions**. Young children may hear a baby cry and try to make the baby feel better. This is the first step in understanding other people's perspectives. As you get older, you can use this understanding to guess what other people are thinking based on their behavior.

CHAPTER FOUR

THEORY OF MIND

When someone understands that other people have their own perspectives, that person has gained **theory** of mind. Having theory of mind means that person can think about and understand how someone else might behave.

Imagine a child and an adult are in a room. The adult puts a toy in a red box and leaves. Then, another adult comes in, takes the toy out of that box, puts it into a blue box, and leaves. The first adult comes back and wants the toy. Which box will they look in?

A child with theory of mind says that the first adult will look in the red box. They understand that the first adult believes the toy is still in the red box even though the child saw someone else put it into the blue box. The child understands the difference between what the first adult believes and what the child knows.

The "red box, blue box" task is called a false-belief test. Someone over age six who can't pass a false-belief test may have **autism**. Some people with autism find it hard to understand how others think.

CHAPTER FIVE

SOCIAL THINKING

Being social means spending time with others. We use social thinking when we communicate with other people. We think about the people around us and what we're going to say. But social thinking isn't just useful when talking. We use social thinking whenever we share space with other people. Moving out of someone's way while you're walking on the sidewalk is social thinking, too!

Social thinking happens all the time. When we're alone, we might think about what we've said to other people. We might wonder if we should have said something different. Social thinking can happen before we meet someone. We imagine what we'll say when we do meet.

Most people want to be liked. Social thinking may cause us to change our behavior so that other people think well of us. Perspective-taking is one way to improve social thinking.

Being a social thinker means remembering that other people decide if they want to be around you based on your actions toward them. If you think you've upset someone, you might say that you're sorry if you want to change their social thinking about you.

CHAPTER SIX

THE OTHER POINT OF VIEW

Perspective-taking means thinking about others and how we're going to act before we speak. It also means knowing the other person is doing the same thing from their perspective.

As soon as two people share space together, they start thinking about each other. What does the other person want? Sometimes, you might guess what someone else is thinking based on their movements or the look on their face. Are their arms crossed? Are they smiling?

We show people how we feel with the way we move our arms, heads, faces, and eyes. This is called body language. How can you tell if someone's sad? What do you think their body language might look like?

Both people may wonder what the other one is thinking: "Has someone told them about me?" "Do they think that I'm a good person?" Each person is aware of how they act. They may change their behavior so that the other person thinks about them in a positive way. Remember, being thoughtful and thinking of someone else's point of view helps you be a better friend.

CHAPTER SEVEN

GREETING GONE WRONG

Here's an example of different perspectives. You see your best friend in the hallway at school. You come up behind them and slap them on the back to say hello. Your friend jumps, then starts yelling. You're shocked at how furious they are. You've clapped your friend on the back hundreds of times. What happened?

Your friend didn't see you at first because their back was turned. Before they turned back around, from their perspective, a stranger just came up and hit them for no reason. Of course your friend was angry!

Because people have different perspectives, it can be easy to **misinterpret** what others do or say. Your friend couldn't see things from your point of view at first. But once they did, they probably weren't angry anymore because they understood that from your perspective, you were just saying hi. Understanding emotions becomes easier when you consider your friend's perspective and they consider yours.

Seeing situations from your friends' perspectives makes for stronger friendships. Consider taking time out of your day to check in and see how some of your friends are feeling.

CHAPTER EIGHT

LIFE LESSONS

Perspective-taking teaches valuable life lessons. Perspective-takers have better relationships with people because they try to understand them. They have more concern and **empathy** for others. They push away bad feelings toward someone by imagining what it would be like to be in their shoes. They think about other people even as they think of themselves and encourage others to do the same.

Imagine a crowd of people exiting a movie theater. Some people thought the movie was the best they'd ever seen! Others hated it. How can people watch the same movie and feel so differently about it? They have their own perspectives.

Perspective-takers aren't **judgmental** toward other people just because they may not look, talk, or think like they do. Having perspective helps us respect people's differences. It teaches us to respect each other even if we don't agree.

Kids who understand other kids' perspectives are more comforting and helpful to each other. They have stronger, longer-lasting friendships. They stand up for other kids who are being bullied.

CHAPTER NINE

GETTING TO KNOW YOUR NEIGHBORS

Do you know anyone you think is rude or **inconsiderate**? They may have trouble with perspective-taking. Maybe they're not thinking about others' feelings before they speak. They may not even understand why others' feelings are hurt.

It's hard to imagine how someone else feels, but it's important to try so we can work together as a community. Perspective-taking helps during disagreements because each person tries to understand the other side and why people with those views feel the way they do. We learn that we can have different ideas and still get along. It's easier to move forward this way because everyone feels respected.

People around the world may have beliefs that you're not familiar with. In Asia, Buddhism is one of the most common religions. Buddhism encourages its followers to find happiness through peace and positivity.

Personal experiences make us who we are. These experiences also shape how we think and act. People with different backgrounds may not see the world the same way. Perspective-taking means putting your own experience aside to figure out how the other person is feeling.

CHAPTER TEN

TAKING PERSPECTIVE OF OUR WORLD

Perspective-taking is a skill that you'll use the rest of your life. When you're working with others as a team, you'll get things done faster because you're able to see things from every side. You'll make decisions more carefully because you'll think about how they affect other people.

Our society is made up of millions of people of different races, religions, and beliefs. Some people won't accept others who are different from them because they refuse to see their point of view. They think less of other people because they don't understand them.

Perspective-takers try to understand what other people are feeling. They keep their own behavior in check so they don't hurt other people. Perspective-takers have an understanding and respect for **diversity**. They celebrate people's differences and keep our society strong.

GLOSSARY

autism (AHW-tih-zuhm) A disorder in which a person may have trouble communicating and socializing with others.

cognitive (KOG-nuh-tiv) Relating to brain activities such as thinking, remembering, or reasoning.

diversity (duh-VUHR-suh-tee) The quality or state of having many different types, forms, or ideas.

emotion (ih-MOH-shuhn) A strong feeling—such as anger, love, joy, or fear—often accompanied by a physical reaction.

empathy (EHM-puh-thee) Being aware of and sharing someone else's feelings.

inconsiderate (ihn-kuhn-SIH-duh-reht) Not thinking of someone else's feelings.

judgmental (juhj-MEHN-tuhl) Judging others, forming an opinion often based on feelings.

misinterpret (miss-uhn-TUHR-pruht) To misunderstand or explain wrongly.

perspective (puhr-SPEK-tiv) Point of view.

psychologist (sy-KAH-luh-jist) A person who studies psychology, or the science or study of the mind and behavior.

theory (THEE-uh-ree) An idea suggested or presented as possibly true but not known or proven to be true.

INDEX

PRIMARY SOURCE LIST

Page 9
Jean Piaget at the University of Michigan campus in Ann Arbor. Photograph. 1967 or 1968. University of Michigan yearbook, *The Michiganensian*, p. 91.

Page 21
Novice monk in a temple in Luang Prabang, Laos. Photograph. Visoot Uthairam. Thailand.

Page 22
Demonstrators at the 2018 March For Our Lives in Washington, D.C. Photograph. Rosa Pineda. March 24, 2018.

WEBSITES

Due to the changing nature of Internet links, PowerKids Press has developed an online list of websites related to the subject of this book. This site is updated regularly. Please use this link to access the list: www.powerkidslinks.com/SSEL/perspective